# The Right Lane to Retirement

## By Michael P. Lane

## Midterm Traders

ISBN: 978-0-6151-4649-2


Published in 2007 by Midterm Traders, Inc.
6300 N. Wickham Rd.
Suite 130
Melbourne, Fl. 32940

mlane@midtermtraders.com
www.justmanageit.com

# Contents

"An idealist is a person who helps other people to be prosperous."

Henry Ford

## Notes

# Disclaimer

*This newly developed **"Retirement Indicator"** is the safest, most profitable way to manage any long-term account. If you wish to get the greatest return with the least amount of risk, read on.*

Past performance is not indicative of future results. Neither Mr. Lane nor Midterm Traders, Inc. guarantees any specific outcome or profit. If you act on our recommendations or opinions without professional advice, you do so at your own risk. Beware of the risk of loss following any strategy. Investors may get back less than they invest.

"What you don't do can be a destructive force."

Eleanor Roosevelt

<u>Notes</u>

# Introduction

You are ready to take control of your financial future. Without any knowledge of the stock market, "The Right Lane to Retirement" will show you how to protect your money while doubling or tripling your long-term returns. With less than five minutes a week and the newly developed *"Retirement Indicator,"* your financial future will be changed forever.

Today, anyone has access to the internet. For this purpose you can pick up a used computer and access the internet for free or use your local library. It's a small price to pay to change your financial future. You're talking about thousands of dollars to protect in just minutes a week. With the *"Retirement Indicator,"* you will know exactly when to protect those dollars and what to do to profit from a down market. For those of you who don't wish to read a chart, go to www.JustManageIt.com and subscribe to this trend service. You will be contacted by e-mail when the trend changes.

If you invested from 01/16/95 through 01/03/07, and you exited when this book said and moved your money into a money market, you would have done very well!

Your gain: +376%

S&P 500: +201%

<u>Notes</u>

What you will learn in the first part of this book is that you have been taught half-truths and myths over the years. You believed in "buy and hold" methods and trusted that someone was managing your personal account on your behalf. Most of you started to question what you were taught during the correction of 2000 when the average portfolios lost forty-six percent. The first thing you found was that you were taught to trust in a financial institution that was not looking out for you, but instead, were looking out for themselves.

Thousands of hours in research and development were needed to find the answers to those questions about long-term investing. Researching the internet, studying historical charts, and back-testing hundreds of indicators was done. It then was discovered that simplicity and common sense were the most common denominators in all of this. With this information, developing a new indicator was the most logical path to take. In the pages ahead, you will discover what was found.

**"Wisdom is what's left after we've run out of personal opinions."**

**Cullen Hightower**

<u>Notes</u>

The *"Retirement Indicator"* is all you need. From this point forward, you should know that your losses that occurred in the past were not your fault; however, now that you will have the information necessary to protect your portfolio, any similar losses in the future will be your fault! You will know exactly when the market trend is up, when it is down, and what you should do to profit from it.

Warren Buffett's number one rule, "never lose the money," truly is the key to growing wealth in the long term. This is exactly what the *"Retirement Indicator"* allows you to do. It shows you exactly when to protect your money, and you will see just how powerful that is when investing for the long term. It will allow you to double or triple your retirement money. It also will allow those who are retired but are running out of money to stay in the market and to continue to grow their retirement account.

It took many years to find something so simple because, everyone is taught that it's complicated and difficult to manage a retirement account. That is the furthest thing from the truth!

**"Facts do not cease to exist because they are ignored."**

**Aldous Huxley**

<u>**Notes**</u>

With advancements of computers, the internet, and online brokers, every individual now has the ability to manage their own account. If you don't, chances are no one else will! A new generation of investors is ready to take charge of their own investments, and this book provides the information needed to do this. The three main objectives are to provide simplicity, affordability, and profitability, which are provided with this book. Now all you have to do is implement the information provided. This could have been written in a 300 page text, taught as a course over 2 months, charging $2,000, but that wasn't the objective. As you read through this book, you will realize that not only is it simple, it's also common sense. *Following the market trend is simple, safe and very profitable!*

Most of the information in the following pages consists of what you should not do. This book is not going to make you a stock trader. You never should trade your retirement account, but you must manage it. The less you know about trading, the easier this is.

"It is our choices… that show what we are far more than our abilities."

J.K. Rowling

Notes

You will learn exactly how to manage your funds stress-free. You will know exactly when to change your portfolio and what to change to. You will be able to double or triple the S&P 500 - something fund managers only dream about. This book will show you exactly how easy it is to manage your money and save thousands of dollars by doing so. It truly is amazing that something so simple can change your life. If you follow the procedures, you will be very happy in your retirement.

Keeping things simple is important. You pick one Mutual Fund to buy when the market is up and one Mutual Fund or money market when the market is down. Write down what fund you will buy when the market trend is up. Then decide if you will move into a money market or buy one of the inverse funds when the market is down.

Example: Market up - buy Rytpx
Market down - buy Rytnx
or
Market down - Money Market

Write your choices down. Keep it simple.

**"There can be no real individual freedom in the presence of economic insecurity."**

**Chester Bowles**

### Notes

# How Much is Enough?

It's important to keep it simple so you can figure this out without any fancy calculators.

## How much do you live on now?

Let's say you live currently on $80,000. You can expect additional income of $30,000 from Social Security, pensions and miscellaneous income upon retirement. You will need 75% of your current income, or in this case, $60,000/year to continue your present standard of living.

Example: $80,000 x .75 = $60,000

$60,000-$30,000 from other income, means you will need $30,000 per year from your retirement account.

Now multiply what you need per year by 22.

Example: $30,000 x 22 = $660,000.00

You will need $660,000, and you should not withdraw more than 5% annually. If you don't have enough, you will have to stay in the market or live on less. You will know how to stay in the market with very low risk.

# "(Common Sense) is the best sense I know of."

## Lord Chesterfield

## <u>Notes</u>

# The Industry and Myths

1. <u>**401k Accounts:**</u> **These are great for making you save money but very poor for providing adequate funds for retirement. The high fees and poor plan choices make it very hard to accumulate the amount of money you will need for retirement. Some estimate that sixty-six percent of the participants will run out of money unless they stay in the stock market. The industry tells us we should reduce our exposure to stocks as we get closer to retirement. With their method of "buy and hold," they're right. But our method provides the safety and protection you will need to stay in the market as long as you need to. Those of you who won't have enough money in retirement can continue to grow your wealth during retirement.**

2. <u>**Buy and Hold:**</u> *"It's okay, you're in it for the long term."* **Has anyone ever heard this one before? What exactly are they saying? It's okay to lose forty-six percent of your portfolio like the last bear market because you have years to make it back? Well it will take years - as many as 5 to 10 years - to get back the losses of the 2000-2001 bear market.**

**"If all economists were laid end to end, they would not reach a conclusion."**

**George Bernard Shaw**

<u>**Notes**</u>

*It never is okay to lose this amount of money in your portfolio, and "buy and hold" is the easiest way to go broke in retirement.* You never should use any method that puts half your money at risk when investing for the long term. The method of "buy and hold" is flawed because it produces low returns and carries a very high risk. "Buy and hold" is obsolete and now is replaced with the *"Retirement Indicator."*

As stated earlier, protecting your money is the key to long-term wealth. Estimates show that sixty-six percent of the people retiring will not have enough money for retirement. That's two out of every three! Now you have the solution to your problem. With the *"Retirement Indicator,"* you can stay in the market after retirement because your money is protected – by you!

If you now are saving for your retirement, always exercise your IRA options. IRA's provide you with choices - something 401k's lack. With these choices and the *"Retirement Indicator,"* you will not be one of the sixty-six percent of the people who run out of money in retirement.

# "Regret for wasted time is more wasted time."

## Mason Cooley

## <u>Notes</u>

3. <u>Diversification</u>: This is very simple. Buy one general and aggressive Mutual Fund, and you will be diversified. Mutual Funds contain hundreds of stocks, making them diversified by nature. Brokers like you to have stock funds, bond funds and money market funds. But stick with just one Mutual Fund. This book will show you how to put all your money to work for you with less risk.

4. <u>Dollar Cost Averaging</u>: Again, great for saving money, but it's not the best way to fund your account. Historically, the best time to increase your stock portfolio is the middle of the September. Has your broker ever told you this?

5. <u>Brokers</u>: In defense of the good people who work in this industry, when the market is in a down trend or correction, they are "between a rock and a hard place." They cannot and will not tell millions of clients to sell everything and get out of the market because the market will crash along with their business. Instead, you can move into cash anytime you want.

**"We find no real satisfaction or happiness in life without obstacles to conquer and goals to achieve."**

**Maxwell Maltz**

<u>**Notes**</u>

This is why you need to be in charge of your own portfolio, because as an individual, you easily can do this with no affect on the market. Those with large portfolios get out of the market while the smaller investor stays around to hold up the bottom of the market. The question here is which one do you want to be? At what point during this last correction did your broker call you to get out? If he didn't, then you need to stop paying him!

If you have an active 401k that you are contributing to, then this is easy. When the market is in a down trend, simply contact the administrator and ask that your money be moved to a money market. Most 401k's and IRA's can be accessed online, and you can make the changes you had previously decided on. If you currently are funding a retirement account, you always should exercise your maximum IRA contribution. IRA accounts provide you with greater choices which will increase your retirement account balance. It is important to understand the benefits of IRA's. Just go to your bank, ask what they offer and how you can manage it.

# "We must use time as a tool, not as a crutch."

## John F. Kennedy

## <u>Notes</u>

# The Retirement Indicator

*It is simple, safe and the most profitable way to manage any long-term account.*

- Simple – Short of doing nothing at all, which can cause devastating losses, it doesn't get any easier. It takes five minutes a month and the ability to know when two lines have crossed.
- Safe – The *"Retirement Indicator"* is flawless and will protect your money. The two lines are moving averages, and moving averages follow the market trend. When the market is going up, they follow the market up until the market rolls over, and the lines cross showing a reversal of the market trend. They allow you to avoid the bear markets like the forty-six percent loss in the last bear market.
- Profitable – This Indicator allows you to be aggressive in a bull market while protecting your principle from a bear market, making it very easy to double your returns. Warren Buffett's number one rule, "never loss the money," is the key to being profitable.

Can you afford to lose 46% again?

**"The advantage of a classical education is that it enables you to despise the wealth which it prevents you from achieving."**

**Russell Green**

**<u>Notes</u>**

SPY (S&P 500 SPDRs) AMEX
31-Dec-2004     Open 114.00 **High** 115.30 **Low** 113.95 **Close** 115.04 **Volume** 51.7M **Chg** +1.29 (+1.14%)

Dow Jones (INDU) - 34%

S&P 500 (SPY) - 46%

Nasdaq 100 (QQQQ) - 54%

Did You Get Out in October 2000?

# Protect your Capital!

## Do you recall this loss in 2000-2001?
## Did anyone call and tell you to get out of the market?

## The overall market lost forty-six percent. The *"Retirement Indicator"* would have saved people thousands of dollars.

**"Not a shred of evidence exists in favor of the idea that life is serious."**

**Brendan Gill**

<u>**Notes**</u>

With your new guide, you would have been out of the market on 10/16/2000. You would have exited on this date and either put your money in a money market or chose one of the inverse bear market choices, which would have made you a nice profit. The Rydex group is used in this book, and the numbers on the graph below shows a fifty-two percent return during this forty-six percent correction or bear market. The vertical lines show our entry and exit points on this trade. As you can see, the trends are long-term trends, and your involvement and time commitment are very small. You can see how powerful it is to make money in a down market!

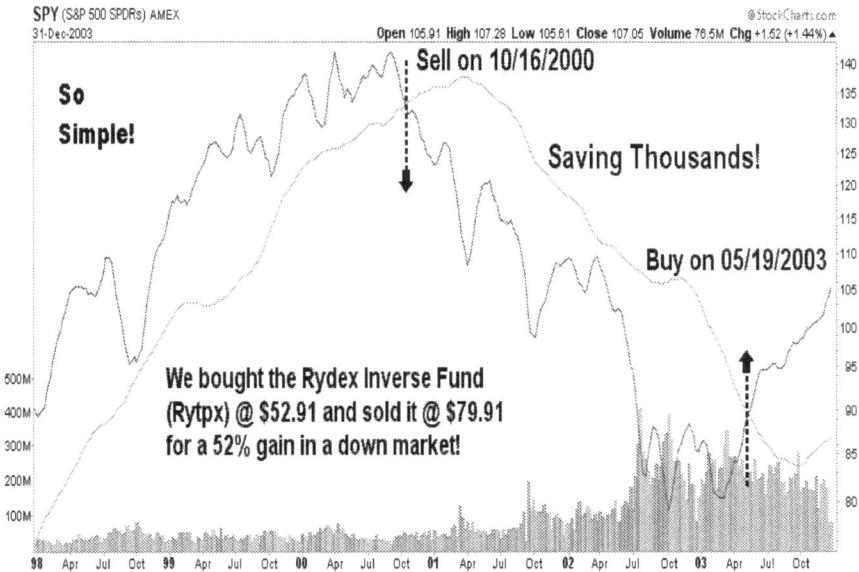

**"I don't know the key to success, but the key to failure is trying to please everyone."**

**Bill Cosby**

**<u>Notes</u>**

The chart below shows the period "since inception" of the S&P 500 index using the tracking ETF (SPY). This index is used for two reasons. It's the one Index all fund managers try to beat, and it's the most accurate predictor of the market. As you can see from this chart, *this method beat the S&P 500 by 175% by simply getting out and moving your money into a money market.* Protecting your principle by avoiding those corrections is the only way to generate wealth! You will never repeat the losses accrued in the 2000 bear market using this indicator.

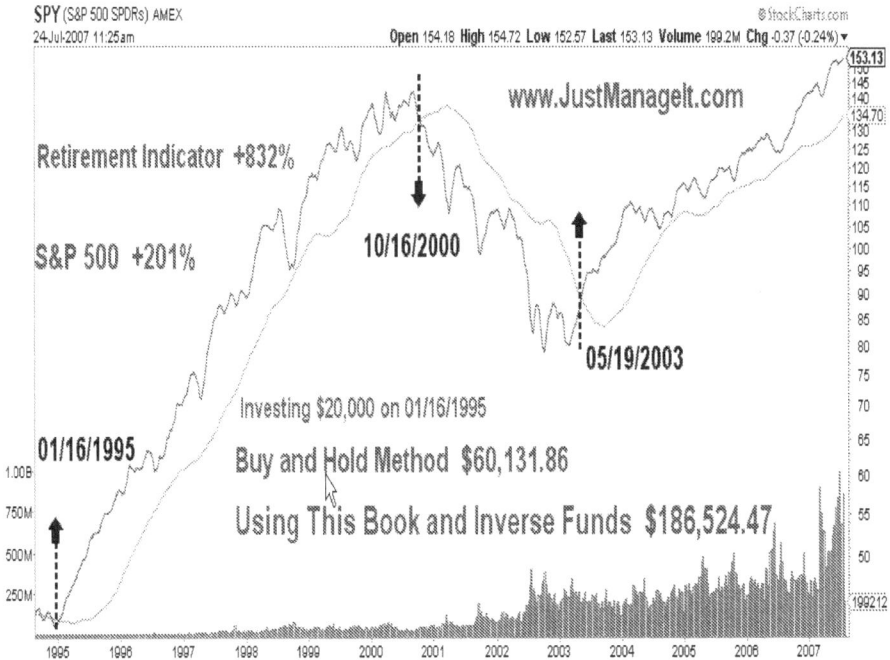

**"Life is tough, and if you have the ability to laugh at it, you have the ability to enjoy it."**

**Salma Hayek**

**Notes**

You can see how easy this new method is. Only three changes in this time period were made. Make sure you either miss the next correction or profit from it.

It is just that easy to out-perform the market when investing for the long term. You have two simple choices, and both are winners for you - either get out and put your money in a money market or buy one of the inverse Mutual Funds.

Remember out of 20,340 Mutual Funds scanned, only four point five percent beat the S&P 500 over the last ten years, and now you will know how to double or triple the S&P 500 yourself! This number shows why "buy and hold" simply does not work. If you buy and hold Mutual Funds, you are looking at being one of the sixty-six percent of the people who will run out of money in your retirement! When someone tells you, *"It's okay, you're in it for the long term,"* ask them why is it okay to lose forty-six percent of my money? They will not know how to answer your question.

**"For myself I am an optimist - it does not seem to be much use being anything else."**

**Sir Winston Churchill**

## Notes

# You're not a stock trader!

This is the Nasdaq-100 weekly chart during the 2000-2001 correction. It is to show you why you suddenly don't think you're a stock trader. This down trend produced a large profit for those who were in a bear market Mutual Fund. You must understand that the market doesn't go up or down in a straight line, so follow your charts, and stay with the rules! The beauty of long-term investing is that you don't have to be concerned with these short-term movements.

SPY (S&P 500 SPDRs) AMEX
28-Feb-2003    Open 80.99 High 81.28 Low 78.41 Close 80.96 Volume 231.8M Chg -0.27 (-0.33%) ▼    ©StockCharts.com

Nine week uptrend in a bear market.

The market never goes up or down in a straight line. Stay with the Retirement Indicator.

**"I have enough money to last the rest of my life, unless I buy something."**

**Jackie Gleason**

**Notes**

Where the trend line is drawn represents a nine week upturn. If you had gotten out of this position before your lines crossed, you would have made a major mistake. This down trend continued for another year. Stay with the big picture and don't think you know what tomorrow will bring. The stock market is very difficult to gauge in the short term. So remember your retirement account never should be traded as a short-term investment.

What makes managing your long-term account so easy is that it doesn't take a lot of time, and you don't have to make many changes. The market doesn't go up or down in a straight line, so remember this is a long-term trend, and the *"Retirement Indicator"* will show you exactly when it's time to take action. For those of you who don't want to spend the time, you can subscribe to receive this trend www.JustManageIt.com. This subscription service provides the trend changes by e-mail. You will know exactly what action is being taken. The two Rydex funds, Rytpx (up market) and the inverse fund or sister fund Rytnx, (down market), are used in this book. There now are many other companies that offer similar funds.

# "Money frees you from doing things you dislike. Since I dislike doing nearly everything, money is handy."

## Groucho Marx

## Notes

# Do not react with emotion!

Tragic events such as 9-11 did and will make the market react. Unless you are on the right side and take profits or you can react before the market, you should sit tight and follow your charts. You must realize that when a tragic event like this occurs, people will rally, and the market will come back. On the chart below, you will see that the market was in a down trend when this tragedy occurred.

SPY (S&P 500 SPDRs) AMEX
31-May-2002          Open 103.17 High 103.24 Low 100.18 Close 101.43 Volume 81.5M Chg -1.39 (-1.35%) ▼

This is the week of Sept. 11th.

Five weeks after the sudden drop, the market recovered.

Five weeks after 9-11, the market moved above where it was on that day. The market then resumed its' previous down trend.

**"A positive attitude may not solve all your problems, but it will annoy enough people to make it worth it."**

**Herm Albright**

<u>**Notes**</u>

# Some Facts

S&P 500–(1/16/95-1/3/07) annualized return +9.64%
## Right Lane +13.93
## With New Inverse Funds +20.52

Out of 20,340 Mutual Funds scanned, only four point five percent were able to meet or beat the S&P 500 over the last ten years. That's just four point five percent of the highly paid, highly educated individuals in the financial industry able to beat this unmanaged index. The ones that did beat the S&P were energy, real estate or emerging market funds. These funds are not even available in most 401k accounts.

Using our favorite S&P 500 Tracking Funds, Rytpx and Rytnx from 01/16/95 - 01/03/07

Retirement Indicator +832%

S&P 500 (SPY) +201%

This is the safest and most profitable way to save for the future. You will be stress-free, retired early, and very happy.

**"In three words I can sum up everything I've learned about life: it goes on."**

**Robert Frost**

**<u>Notes</u>**

# Example # 1

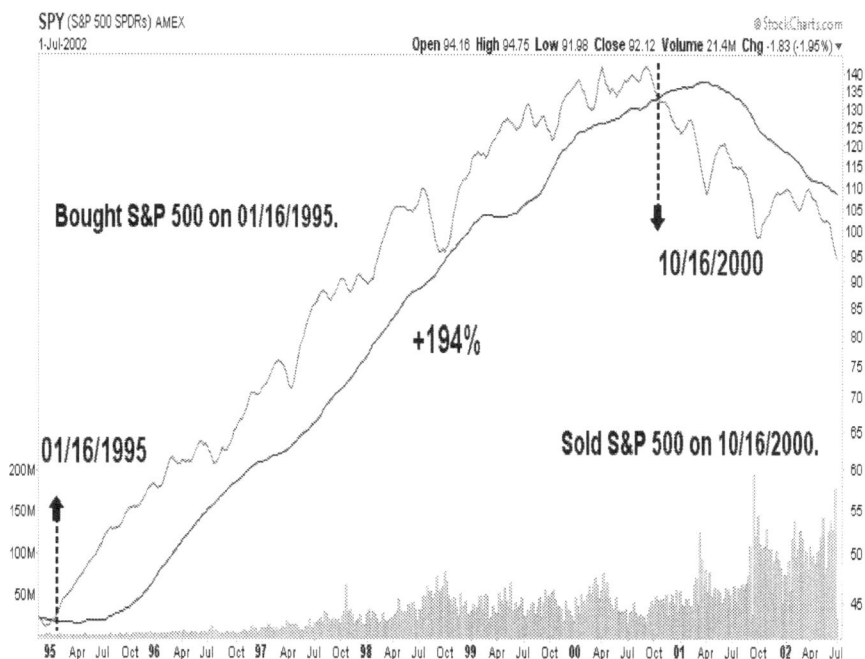

SPY (S&P 500 SPDRs) AMEX
1-Jul-2002
Open 94.16 High 94.75 Low 91.98 Close 92.12 Volume 21.4M Chg -1.83 (-1.95%) ▼
@ StockCharts.com

Bought S&P 500 on 01/16/1995.

+194%

01/16/1995

10/16/2000

Sold S&P 500 on 10/16/2000.

This is the first trade of the S&P 500.

Here you see the market line (jagged) is crossing the trend line (smooth) on 01/16/1995. Follow the market line. In this case, the market is up (Bullish); therefore, buy the S&P 500 Index. (SPY)

Then sell SPY on 10/16/2000 when the market line crosses over the trend line for a *hundred and ninety-four percent gain!* In 1995, the special inverse funds that doubled were not available; however, there are many inverse funds available today.

**"Motivation is what gets you started; habit is what keeps you going."**

**Jim Ryum**

**<u>Notes</u>**

# Example # 2

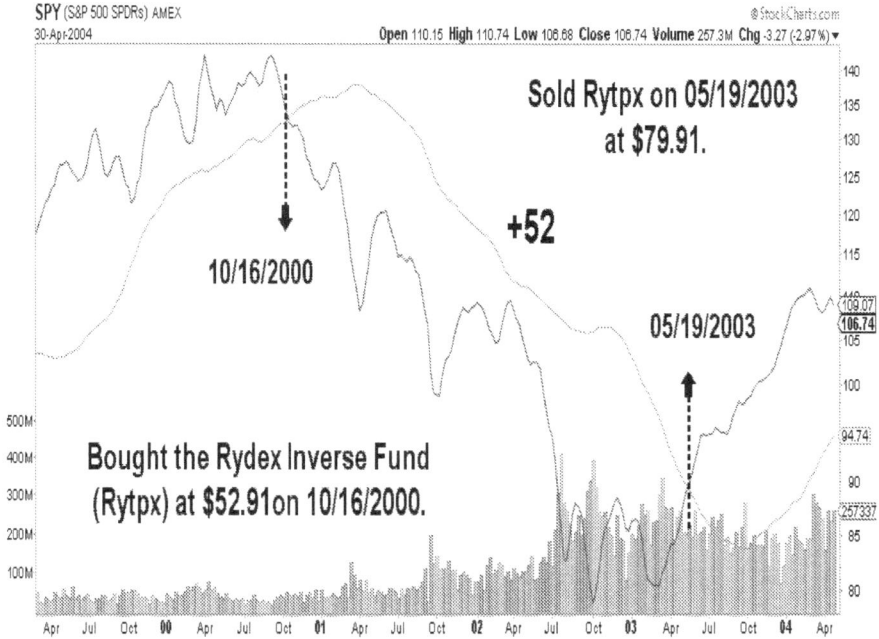

SPY (S&P 500 SPDRs) AMEX
30-Apr-2004
Open 110.15 High 110.74 Low 106.68 Close 106.74 Volume 257.3M Chg -3.27 (-2.97%) ▼
© StockCharts.com

Sold Rytpx on 05/19/2003 at $79.91.

+52

10/16/2000

05/19/2003

Bought the Rydex Inverse Fund (Rytpx) at $52.91 on 10/16/2000.

Do you see how easy this is? You simply follow the market line. When the market line crosses the trend line, you make your changes. Check your chart as often as you like, and never assume the lines will cross!

One of the new Mutual Funds now available to profit from a down market. These funds go up when the market is going down. While many people were losing their money, this method gained fifty-two percent. This is how you catch up your account or just increase your profits.

**"Obstacles are those frightful things you see when you take your eyes off your goals."**

**Henry Ford**

## <u>Notes</u>

# Example # 3

SPY (S&P 500 SPDRs) AMEX
20-Jul-2007                          Open 150.87 High 156.00 Low 150.52 Close 153.50 Volume 1.9B Chg +3.24 (+2.16%) ▲

Never assume the lines are going to cross.

Take action only when the lines have crossed on the weekend.

Check your chart on the weekend and never act unless the lines have crossed. *Never assume anything.* This book is designed to show you exactly when to act. You will see that this chart moves very slow. When the lines are far apart you will see that no action will be needed right away. If you check them every weekend, then you will know your money is safe.

**"The important thing is not to stop questioning."**

**Albert Einstein**

## Notes

# How it Works

**Go to:** *http://www.stockcharts.com*

**Right now the chart you need is free. If that changes, check our site or subscribe. A subscription to this site is recommended.**

- **In the box,** *Easy as 1-2-3***, Enter the symbol,** *SPY* **and click** *Go***.**

- **Scroll down below the chart to** *Chart Attributes***, under** *Periods***, click the drop down menu and select** *Weekly***. To the right click the drop down menu under range and select** *three years.*

- **Next scroll down under** *type***, click the drop down menu and select** *Invisible***. Across to** *Size* **select** *700.*

- **Move down to** *Overlays***, across from** *Simple Mov. Avg.* **remove the** *50* **and type in** *31,25***. (that's 31 coma 25) Move down to the next** *Simple Mov. Avg.* **remove the** *200* **and type in** *4.*

- **Under** *Indicators* **click the drop down menus and click** *none***. Now click** *Update***.**

35

# "It is a miracle that curiosity survives formal education."

**Albert Einstein**

## <u>Notes</u>

Now you have your chart and you can see just how easy it is. Simply follow the market line (jagged). If you had any trouble setting up this chart, look below to see how it should look before you click update. If you do sign up for this site, you can save the chart and it will update automatically.

*Michael P. Lane*

# "What you don't do can be a destructive force."

## Eleanor Roosevelt

### Notes

If you have any questions, please go to our website  *www.justmanageit.com*  or e-mail us service@midtermtraders.com

For long-term investing, this is all you need to avoid the bear market and profit from the bull market. Most of you have 401k's, so your choices will be limited. Buy the funds when the market is up, and move into a money market when the market is down. Try to exercise your IRA options each year, then you can buy any Mutual Fund at anytime. These accounts have very few rules compared to 401k plans. You will be able to profit when the market is down by using the funds that are mentioned. If you change jobs, roll your 401k into an IRA at your bank and elect to manage it yourself. Your bank will make the transfer for you. If your bank can not take care of it for you, then shop around for what you need. If you have more than one IRA, put them together. It will save you money.

"When one door closes another door opens; but we so often look so long and so regretfully upon the closed door, that we do not see the ones which open for us.

**Alexander Graham Bell**

<u>**Notes**</u>

If you have a private account or an IRA, you can manage your own account and choose any of the choices available. If you like to be more active and buy stocks, do it in a separate account. Buying stocks in a retirement account requires a big time commitment on your part. You must be diversified to reduce risk. Mutual Funds used as a tool for long-term investing are diversified and carry much less risk. The new funds which double the market movements are very profitable.

Most people who have retired with a 401k still are paying very high fees. You can have that money rolled over into an IRA account at your local bank and control it yourself. They will move your money and show you how easy it is to manage it yourself. Remember there are very few changes to make. If you just manage it yourself, you will save some of the fees charged. We all have been taught how difficult this is and that it should be left to a professional. The truth is, the professional you thought manages your money doesn't, and it is simple to do yourself, so just do it now!

# "Perpetual optimism is a force multiplier."

## Colin Powell

## <u>Notes</u>

# Reading Your Chart

Follow the market (jagged) line. When that line crosses below the trend (smooth) line, the trend is down. When that line crosses above the trend line, the trend is up.

This is a weekly chart, so you read them on the weekend. Check the chart after the close of the market on the final day of the week. Take action when the market line has crossed the trend line. Because this is long-term trading, you will see that things move slowly, and you won't have to be checking every week once you become familiar with it. The market goes up most of the time.

This is the easiest and most profitable way for you to invest in the market for the long term. It takes only the ability to act to beat most fund managers in the industry. Remember, only four point five percent of them beat the S&P 500, and you can double or triple this index yourself just by protecting your money. With the *"Retirement Indicator"*, you will be protected before and after retirement.

# "Many an optimist has become rich by buying out a pessimist."

### Robert G. Allen

## Notes

If you chart some funds over the last ten years, you will see that they basically corrected the same as the S&P 500.

Above is the S&P 500 during the 2000-2001 correction. The average market corrected 46% along with the S&P 500.

Above is the largest US stock market Mutual Fund, with an overall Morningstar rating of five stars. It corrected 45.9% during the 2000-2001 bear market.

**"A man can't be always defending the truth; there must be a time for him to feed on it."**

**C.S Lewis**

**<u>Notes</u>**

If you are paying a fee for someone to manage your portfolio, you must ask yourself if they actually are managing it for you. Did they get you out in Oct. 2000? If not, you may be paying them to simply hold your money, in which case you should have it transferred to your bank and control it yourself! The fees that are charged for someone to hold your money will reduce your retirement account.

Six years is much time to lose when you are trying to build a portfolio for your retirement. There is no reason to lose this time, and the Retirement Indicator will prevent it.

# "Life consists not in holding good cards but in playing those cards well."

**Josh Billings**

## Notes

# When the Trend is Up
## (bull market options)

## Special Mutual Funds:

- **Buy the RYVYX Mutual Fund. It doubles the** NASDAQ 100.

- **Buy** RYTNX **which tracks the** S&P 500 **and doubles the change in this index.**

- **Buy** RYRSX **which tracks the** Russell 2000 **and will double the change in this index.**

**The funds that double are preferred, as well as buying one Mutual Fund. Here are some funds that match the index they follow. You must decide if you want to match, double or just buy one of the funds you have already. Remember these are Mutual Funds, and your money is very safe due to the nature of trend trading. The stock market is the best place to be when you know which way it's going!**

- RYOCX **matches the** Nasdaq 100
- BLPIX **matches the** S&P 500
- SLPIX **matches the** Russell 2000

*Michael P. Lane*

# "A dream becomes a goal when action is taken towards its' achievement."

## Bo Bennett

## <u>Notes</u>

# Mutual Funds

Buy the fund of your choice as long as it's a bull market fund, which most are. Funds are much safer than individual stocks because they are made up of hundreds of stocks. Many people with 401k's don't have a lot of choices, so buy the most aggressive fund available. Remember if you exercise your IRA option, you will have unlimited choices.

# Index ETF's

- **QQQQ tracks the NASDAQ**
- **SPY tracks the S&P 500**
- **DIA tracks the Dow Jones**

There are 1000's of exchange-traded funds (ETF's). If you know them and like to trade them, then buy them when the market is up. The special Mutual Funds are preferred over the Index's and ETF's. If you choose to buy ETF's, remember you need to be diversified. If you purchase the S&P 500 (SPY), you will be diversified. If you purchase sectors, you must be familiar with what you are doing and purchase four or five sectors.

**"People are just as happy as they make up their minds to be."**

**Abraham Lincoln**

<u>**Notes**</u>

# When the Trend is Down
## (Bear market options)

# Money Markets

These are for those who don't have inverse funds available or choose not to trade the market to the downside but wish to avoid the loss. Sell your fund and put all your money in the money market available. It's a very safe and secure place to have your money when the market is going down.

# Special Mutual Funds

- Buy the RYVNX Mutual Fund. This doubles the NASDAQ 100 in the opposite direction. When the market is going down, this fund goes up.

- Buy the RYTPX Mutual Fund. This doubles the S&P 500 in the opposite direction. Again, when the market is going down, this fund goes up.

- Buy RYIRX. This fund tracks the Russell 2000 and doubles in the opposite direction. Again, when the market is going down, this fund goes up.

**"The constitution only gives people the right to pursue happiness. You have to catch it yourself."**

**Ben Franklin**

<u>**Notes**</u>

# Gold ETF or Gold Bullion

Gold and gold stocks normally move in the opposite direction of the stock market and the US dollar. The new gold ETF Index trades under the symbol GLD. This market has changed in the last three to five years and is not as consistent, but it still is used as a defensive play.

## Remember

When inverse funds double a certain index, you must take in consideration the price of each. If the index costs $40 and the fund costs $20, then the daily movement needs to be only equal to double.

People who feel they might not have enough money to retire and need to catch up now have the tools to do it. It is very important that you open an IRA and manage it yourself. Use the funds that double and catch up. Do not consider these special funds' performance over the long term. Use these funds only as a tool. When the market is up, buy one fund, and when the market is down, buy the inverse fund or sister fund.

**"He who asks a question is a fool for five minutes; he who does not ask a question remains a fool forever."**

**Chinese Proverb**

<u>**Notes**</u>

# Let's Review

1) Always follow the market (jagged) line. When it crosses the trend line, you make changes. When the market line crosses going down, the market is down (bearish). When the market line crosses going up, the market is going up (bullish).

2) Check weekly charts only on the weekend. There is nothing to learn and no long hours of study. Just follow the line.

3) Now you know how easy it is to protect your money which will double or triple your retirement account. People who have IRA's or personal accounts now can take advantage of the new funds that double the market going up or down. This will more than triple your retirement account.

# As simple as that!

**Never assume the lines will cross.**

"Learning is about more than simply acquiring new knowledge and insight; it is also crucial to unlearn old knowledge that has outlived its relevance. Thus, forgetting is probably at least as important as learning."

Gary Ryan Blair

<u>Notes</u>

Let's look and compare a fund that doubles the market movement. Below is a chart of the present bull market. The S&P 500 shows a sixty-seven percent rise over this four year period.

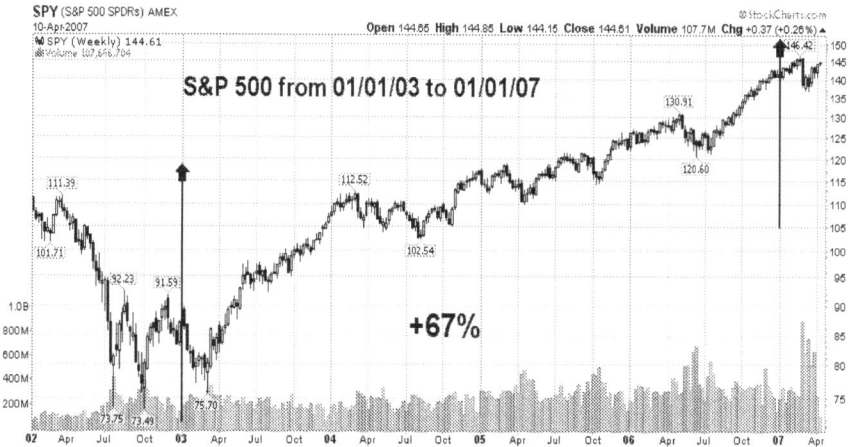

S&P 500 from 01/01/03 to 01/01/07

+67%

Rydex (Ryvyx) from 01/01/03 to 01/01/07

+141%

During the same time period the Rydex Fund was up one hundred and forty-one percent.

**"Change your thoughts and you change your world."**

**Norman Vincent Peale**

<u>**Notes**</u>

# Getting Started

Once you have read through this material and set up your chart, you are ready to get started. If the weekly chart is moving up (the market line is above the trend line), then you can stay with the funds you now have or buy one of the more aggressive funds. To keep things simple, you should write down your one choice for an up market and your choice of a money market or an inverse Mutual Fund for a down market.

As stated earlier, it is recommended that you buy one fund. Some people like to watch these special funds to get a feel for how they work. Do what is comfortable for you. This should be stress-free. These are decisions you will have to make. Remember you are buying a Mutual Fund which contains hundreds of stocks, and you actively are protecting your money!

If you are new, it is recommended that you change your position (go into the money market or inverse fund) if the jagged line is below the smooth line. Remember, these are long-term trends, so protect your money now.

If you have any questions, go to our website and e-mail us.

# Michael P. Lane
## President: Midterm Traders
## www.justmanageit.com

# Conclusion

The best way to accumulate enough money for retirement is to follow this book. You need to do two things: be very aggressive and protect your money. You have been shown how to do both. Whether you are saving for the future or you need to stay in the market after you have retired, this is "The Right Lane to Retirement."

Buy one general Mutual Fund which will make you diversified. Protect your money by checking your weekly chart using the *"Retirement Indicator."* If you need to be more aggressive, buy a special fund that doubles the market. Use the inverse funds that doubles when the market goes down.

If you don't have an IRA account, you need to start one today! Those of you who are paying someone to "manage" your account need to look at this and decide if it's worth it. Spending the little time it takes to manage your own retirement will pay off in the end.

# "Knowing is not enough; we must apply!

### Goethe

### <u>Notes</u>

# Favorite Web Sites

## Trend Service:

www.JustManageIt.com

## Best Stock Charts:

www.stockcharts.com

## Best Online Broker:

www.optionsxpress.com

## Research:

www.smartmoney.com
www.stockcharts.com

## Best Analyst:

Jim Cramer

**"History will be kind to me for I intend to write it."**

**Sir Winston Churchill**

## <u>Notes</u>

# The Right Lane to Retirement
## Dollar Return: Starting with $20,000

### "Buy and Hold" – How to go broke.

01/16/1995---01/03/2007                    **+201%**

Portfolio Balance:          **$60,131.86**
Annualized Return:                          **9.64%**

------------

### "Retirement Indicator" – Enter money market (2.483%) during down market.

01/16/1995---01/03/2007                    **+376%**

Portfolio Balance:          **$95,171.04**
Annualized Return:                          **13.93%**

------------

### "Retirement Indicator" – Using special Rydex funds as of 2000. (Rytpx,Rytnx)

01/16/1995---01/03/2007                    **+802%**

Portfolio Balance:          **$180,344.69**
Annualized Return:                          **20.18%**

All figures used are from Bigcharts historical quotes.

# "Your success depends only on your actions."

## Michael P. Lane

## <u>Notes</u>

*Enjoy Life*

*&*

*Enjoy Retirement*

All charts are courtesy of Stockcharts

www.stockcharts.com

**"It's not your blue blood, your pedigree or your college degree. It's what you do with your life that counts."**

**Millard Fuller**

**<u>Notes</u>**

# ORDER BOOKS FOR FRIENDS AND FAMILY!

## Order two and get one free!
## Plus free shipping!

## Keep updated with any changes
## by registering at:

## www.JustManageIt.com

## simply send an e-mail with 'register' typed
## in the subject column.